# Money Talks

## *A Financial Guide for Young Adults*

Darrel Francis Jr., MBA

ISBN 978-0-9997372-2-4

# Dedication

To the next generation —

The ones determined to do better, build smarter, and break cycles.

To the young adults who were never taught how money really works,
but decided to learn anyway.

To the families working hard every day,
hoping the next generation goes further.

To my family —
for the lessons, the sacrifices, and the vision of something greater.

My Wife Courtney, My Kids Darrel III, Darren, Amari, Mahlea and Dylan…

And my adorable grand-daughter LaeLa :)

This book is for the builders.
The thinkers.
The planners.
The disciplined ones.

May you build wealth that creates freedom,
and freedom that creates legacy.

# Foreword

Financial literacy is not a luxury skill.

It is a survival skill.

For too long, essential money conversations have been missing from classrooms, dinner tables, and communities. Young adults graduate knowing how to pass exams — but not how to manage a paycheck. They understand history and science — but not credit, investing, debt, or wealth-building.

The consequences are real:

- High-interest debt
- Financial stress
- Poor credit decisions

- Delayed wealth-building
- Generational cycles of instability

But the solution is simple:

Education.

This book does not promise quick money.
It does not promise shortcuts.

It provides something far more powerful:

Understanding.

When young adults understand income, budgeting, credit, investing, and ownership, they gain more than knowledge — they gain control.

Financial control reduces stress.
Financial stability increases options.
Financial literacy builds freedom.

The information in this book can shift not only individual lives — but entire families.

The earlier these lessons are learned, the stronger the foundation becomes.

# Introduction: Why Nobody Taught You This

You probably learned:

How to solve equations.
How to write essays.
How to memorize historical dates.

But you probably were not taught:

How to read a paycheck.
How credit scores work.
How interest compounds.
How to invest.
How to build assets.

Why?

Because financial education has never been consistently prioritized.

Many adults were never taught these lessons themselves.
So they couldn't pass them down.

Financial literacy gaps are rarely intentional.
They are inherited.

Schools often focus on standardized testing.
Families focus on survival.
Communities focus on immediate needs.

But money quietly affects everything:

- Where you live
- The stress you carry
- The opportunities you can pursue
- The risks you can take

- The legacy you leave

When financial education is missing, people learn through mistakes.

Expensive mistakes.

This book exists so you don't have to learn everything the hard way.

It gives you:

- The rules of income
- The structure of budgeting
- The truth about credit
- The strategy behind investing
- The power of ownership
- The mindset required to build wealth

You don't need to be born wealthy.

You need to be informed.

Financial literacy is not about becoming rich overnight.

It's about making intentional decisions that strengthen your future.

No one may have taught you before.

But you can learn now.

And you can pass it forward.

# How to Use This Book

This book is not meant to be skimmed.

It is meant to be applied.

Here is how to get the most from it:

## 1. Read in Order

Each chapter builds on the previous one.

Mindset → Income → Budget → Credit → Debt → Investing → Ownership.

Skipping foundations weakens strategy.

## 2. Complete the Reflection Questions

At the end of each chapter, you'll find reflection questions.

Don't skip them.

Write your answers.

Awareness creates clarity.
Clarity creates action.

## 3. Apply One Concept at a Time

You do not need to change everything overnight.

Start with:

- Building a starter emergency fund
- Tracking your spending
- Checking your credit score
- Opening an investment account

Small actions create momentum.

Momentum builds confidence.

## 4. Revisit Annually

Your income will change.
Your goals will evolve.
Your responsibilities will grow.

Revisit this book each year.

Financial growth requires ongoing awareness.

## 5. Teach What You Learn

The ultimate sign of understanding is teaching.

Share these principles with:

- Siblings

- Friends
- Children
- Family members

When you teach financial literacy, you multiply its impact.

# Final Word Before You Begin

You do not need perfection.

You need direction.

Wealth is not built in one decision.

It is built in consistent decisions over time.

The goal of this book is not to impress you.

It is to equip you.

Read it carefully.
Apply it intentionally.
Build strategically.

Your future self is depending on the choices you make now.

# Part I: The Foundation – How Money Really Works

## Chapter 1: Money Mindset — The Way You Think Shapes the Way You Earn

Scarcity vs. Abundance Thinking
Delayed Gratification
Discipline Over Motivation
Financial Identity
Breaking Generational Money Habits

## Chapter 2: Understanding Income — How Money Comes In

Active vs. Passive Income
Jobs vs. Careers vs. Entrepreneurship
Reading a Paycheck Stub
Gross vs. Net Pay
Taxes Explained Simply

# Part II: Managing Money Like an Adult

## Chapter 3: Budget Like a Boss

Why Most Budgets Fail
The 50/30/20 Rule
Zero-Based Budgeting
Digital Budget Tools
Avoiding Lifestyle Inflation

# Part V: Big Financial Decisions

## Chapter 10: Insurance & Protection



## Chapter 11: Adult Milestones — Cars, Apartments & First Homes



# Part VI: Legacy & Long-Term Strategy

## Chapter 12: Wealth, Ownership & Generational Impact

Assets vs. Liabilities
Real Estate Basics
Ownership Mindset
Building a 10-Year Plan
Teaching the Next Generation

CHAPTER 1

# MONEY MINDSET

## The Way You Think Shapes the Way You Earn

# Chapter 1: Money Mindset — The Way You Think Shapes the Way You Earn

Most people don't have a money problem. They have a thinking problem. Before we talk about credit scores, investing, or budgeting apps, we need to talk about mindset — because the way you think about money determines how you handle it.
If you believe money is hard to earn, it will be.
If you believe you'll "figure it out later," you probably won't.
If you believe wealth is only for certain people, you'll unconsciously block yourself from building it.
Money responds to discipline, awareness, and strategy — not luck.

## Scarcity vs. Abundance Thinking

There are two dominant financial mindsets:

### 1. Scarcity Mindset

- "I'll never make enough."
- "Rich people are greedy."
- "I just need to get by."
- "Money always runs out."

Scarcity thinking leads to:

- Living paycheck to paycheck
- Fear-based decisions

Avoiding investing
Avoiding risks that lead to growth

**2. Abundance Mindset**

"I can increase my income."
"Skills can be monetized."
"Money is a tool."
"I can learn what I don't know."

Abundance thinking leads to:

Seeking opportunities
Learning new skills
Strategic risk-taking
Long-term wealth building

The truth? Most young adults were never taught abundance thinking around money. They were taught survival.
But survival is not wealth.

## Delayed Gratification: The Superpower

One of the biggest predictors of financial success is the ability to delay gratification.
In simple terms:
Can you say no now so you can say yes later?
Examples:

Not upgrading your phone every year
Not financing rims before you have savings
Not spending your entire tax refund
Not buying designer just to impress

Delayed gratification creates:

- Savings
- Investment capital
- Options
- Freedom

The people who look “rich” early often look stressed later.
The people who look disciplined early often look wealthy later.

## Financial Identity: Who Are You Becoming?

You don’t rise to the level of your goals.
You rise to the level of your identity.
If you see yourself as:

- “Bad with money”
- “A spender”
- “Someone who can’t save”

You will unconsciously prove yourself right.

Instead, start asking:

- What would a financially responsible adult do?
- What would an investor do?
- What would a future homeowner do?

Shift from:
“I’m trying to save.”
To:
“I’m becoming someone who builds wealth.”
Identity drives behavior.

## Breaking Generational Money Habits

Every family has money habits.
Some are helpful:

- Working hard
- Avoiding unnecessary debt
- Living below means

Some are harmful:

- Avoiding investing out of fear
- Normalizing paycheck-to-paycheck living
- Avoiding financial conversations
- Believing wealth is “not for us”

Breaking generational habits does not mean disrespecting your upbringing.
It means upgrading it.
You can honor where you come from while improving where you’re going.

## Discipline Over Motivation

Motivation fades.
Discipline remains.
You will not always *feel* like budgeting.
You will not always *feel* like saving.
You will not always *feel* like investing.
Financial success is not emotional.
It is systematic.
Wealth is built through boring consistency:

- Automatic transfers
- Scheduled investments
- Monthly check-ins

Intentional spending
Boring builds wealth.

## The Truth About Income

Here's something important:
Income alone does not create wealth.
There are people making $40,000 with savings.
There are people making $400,000 living paycheck to paycheck.
Wealth is not what you earn.
It's what you keep.
It's what you grow.
It's what you own.

## The Freedom Formula

Money equals options.
Options equal freedom.
When you:

Have savings → You can leave bad situations.

Have investments → You can grow without constant labor.

Have low debt → You can make bold moves.

Money does not buy happiness.
But lack of money creates stress.
Financial literacy reduces stress.

## Reflection Questions

What beliefs about money did I grow up hearing?
Are those beliefs helping or limiting me?
What kind of financial adult do I want to become?
What is one habit I can improve this month?

## Chapter Takeaway

Before you manage money, you must manage your mindset.
You don't build wealth accidentally.
You build it intentionally.
And intention begins with how you think.

CHAPTER 2

# UNDERSTANDING INCOME

— How Money Comes In

# Chapter 2: Understanding Income — How Money Comes In

Before you can manage money, you have to understand how it actually enters your life.

Most young adults focus on what they want to buy.

Very few focus on how money is created.

Income is the engine of your financial life.
But not all income is created equal.

If you misunderstand income, you will mismanage everything else.

## The Three Ways Money Comes In

There are only three primary ways to earn money:

### 1. Active Income

This is money you earn by trading time for dollars.

Examples:

- Hourly jobs
- Salaried positions
- Overtime
- Freelancing

If you stop working, the income stops.

Active income is where almost everyone begins — and that's okay.

But understand this:
Active income alone rarely creates wealth.

### 2. Leveraged Income

This is income earned through systems, teams, or scalable work.

Examples:

- Owning a business with employees
- Selling digital products
- Running an online store

- Monetized content

Your time is not directly tied to every dollar earned.

This is where income begins to expand beyond your personal hours.

### 3. Passive Income

This is income that continues with minimal daily effort.

Examples:

- Rental income
- Dividends from investments
- Royalties
- Interest from savings

Passive income requires work upfront — but pays you long-term.

Most wealthy individuals don’t rely on just one type of income.

They combine all three.

## Jobs vs. Careers vs. Entrepreneurship

Understanding income also means understanding your path.

### A Job

- Pays for your time
- Usually hourly
- Flexible but limited growth
- Often short-term

A job can build discipline, work ethic, and initial savings.

### A Career

- Skill-based

- Higher income ceiling
- Long-term growth
- Benefits (insurance, retirement plans)

Careers require education, certifications, or trade skills.

**Entrepreneurship**

- Unlimited income potential
- Higher risk
- Requires self-discipline
- Builds assets

Entrepreneurship is not “quick money.”
It’s ownership.

Ownership builds wealth.

## Gross Pay vs. Net Pay: The Shock Most Young Adults Face

When you first receive a job offer, you may see:

"$50,000 per year."

That is **gross pay** — before taxes.

What actually hits your bank account is **net pay** — after taxes and deductions.

Typical deductions include:

- Federal taxes
- State taxes
- Social Security
- Medicare
- Health insurance
- Retirement contributions

Your real spendable income is your net pay.

If you budget using gross income, you will overspend.

# Reading a Paycheck Stub

Most people never look closely at their paycheck breakdown.

That's a mistake.

A paycheck stub shows:

- Gross income
- Taxes withheld
- Insurance deductions
- Retirement contributions
- Net pay
- Year-to-date totals

Understanding this helps you:

- Estimate your real monthly income
- Adjust tax withholdings
- See how much you're saving for retirement
- Avoid tax surprises

Income literacy is adult literacy.

## W-2 vs. 1099: Why It Matters

There are two common classifications for workers:

### W-2 Employee

- Taxes automatically withheld
- Employer may provide benefits
- More stability

### 1099 Contractor

- No taxes withheld automatically
- Must pay quarterly estimated taxes
- More flexibility
- Higher responsibility

Many young adults get excited about 1099 income because the checks look bigger.

But if you don't set aside 20–30% for taxes, that "big check" can become a big tax bill.

Income is not what you receive.
It's what you keep after obligations.

## Increasing Income: The Real Strategy

Budgeting alone won't make you wealthy.

At some point, you must increase income.

Here are strategic ways to grow it:

### 1. Increase Your Skills

Higher skills = higher pay.

Certifications.
Trade skills.
Technology.
Financial literacy.
Communication.

Income follows value.

### 2. Negotiate

Most people never negotiate salary.

Over a lifetime, that costs hundreds of thousands of dollars.

You are paid based on:

- Value delivered
- Market demand
- Confidence displayed

Learn to ask.

### 3. Add a Second Stream

Side income accelerates wealth-building.

Examples:

- Tutoring
- Freelance services

- Reselling
- Digital products
- Consulting
- Creative services

One income covers bills.

Multiple incomes build wealth.

## The Income Trap

As income increases, so does lifestyle.

New job → New car.

Raise → New apartment.

Bonus → Vacation.

This is called **lifestyle inflation**.

If your expenses rise as fast as your income, you stay stuck.

The goal is:

Increase income.
Increase investments.
Increase assets.
Not just increase spending.

## Income and Freedom

Income creates options.

Options create leverage.

Leverage creates freedom.

When you understand how income works:

- You make smarter career decisions.
- You avoid tax surprises.
- You build multiple streams.
- You increase confidence.

Financial independence begins with income awareness.

## Reflection Questions

1. What type of income do I currently earn?
2. How many income streams do I have?
3. Do I understand my paycheck deductions?
4. What skill could I develop that would increase my income within 12 months?

## Chapter Takeaway

Income is not just about making money.

It's about understanding:

- Where it comes from
- Where it goes
- How to increase it
- How to protect it

You don't need to start rich. But you do need to start informed.

CHAPTER 3
BUDGET LIKE A BOSS
INCOME
JOBS
SIDE HUSTLES
GOALS
• SAVE
• SPEND
• INVEST
GOALS
SAVE
SPEND
INVEST
BUDGET
INCOME
EXPENSES
SAVINGS

# Chapter 3: Budget Like a Boss

Most people say they "have a budget."

What they really have is a list of bills.

A real budget is not a restriction.
It's a strategy.

It tells your money where to go instead of wondering where it went.

If income is the engine, budgeting is the steering wheel.

Without it, you might be moving — but you're not in control.

## Why Most Budgets Fail

Budgeting fails for three common reasons:

1. **It's unrealistic.**
   People create strict budgets they can't sustain.

2. **It's not tracked.**
   A budget written once and ignored is useless.

3. **It doesn't include real life.**
   Fun, eating out, and entertainment must be accounted for.

A good budget is honest.
A great budget is flexible but disciplined.

## Step One: Know Your Real Numbers

Before creating a budget, answer three questions:

1. What is my monthly net income?

2. What are my fixed expenses?

3. What are my variable expenses?

### Fixed Expenses

These stay mostly the same:

- Rent

- Car payment
- Insurance
- Phone bill
- Subscriptions

### Variable Expenses

These change month to month:

- Groceries
- Gas
- Dining out
- Shopping
- Entertainment

You can’t control what you don’t measure.

Track one full month before making major changes.

## The 50/30/20 Rule

One of the simplest budgeting frameworks is:

- **50% Needs**
- **30% Wants**
- **20% Savings/Investments**

**50% — Needs**

Essentials:

- Housing
- Utilities
- Insurance
- Minimum debt payments
- Transportation

**30% — Wants**

Lifestyle:

- Dining out
- Streaming services

- Travel
- Hobbies
- Shopping

**20% — Savings & Investments**

- Emergency fund
- Retirement
- Investing
- Extra debt payments

This rule works well for beginners because it's simple and balanced.

But it's not one-size-fits-all.

If your income is lower, you may need:

- 60% Needs
- 20% Wants
- 20% Savings

The goal is intentional allocation — not perfection.

## Zero-Based Budgeting: Every Dollar Has a Job

In zero-based budgeting, your income minus expenses equals zero.

That doesn't mean you spend everything.

It means every dollar is assigned:

Income: $3,000

- Rent: $1,000
- Utilities: $200
- Car: $400
- Insurance: $200
- Groceries: $400
- Gas: $150
- Savings: $400
- Investments: $250

Remaining: $0

Nothing is left unplanned.

Zero-based budgeting builds discipline and awareness.

## The Power of Paying Yourself First

Most people do this:

Spend → Save What's Left

Successful people do this:

Save → Spend What's Left

Set up automatic transfers:

- 10–20% to savings
- Automatic investment contributions

- Automatic retirement deposits

Automation removes emotion.

Emotion ruins budgets.

## Avoiding Lifestyle Inflation

When income increases, most people upgrade immediately:

- New car
- Bigger apartment
- Designer brands
- More subscriptions

That upgrade becomes your new normal.

And you're still broke — just at a higher level.

Instead:

- Increase savings rate
- Increase investment contributions

- Increase asset purchases

Let your lifestyle grow slowly.
Let your assets grow quickly.

## Common Budget Mistakes

1. Ignoring small purchases ("It's just $10.")
2. Forgetting annual expenses (car registration, gifts, holidays)
3. Underestimating groceries
4. Not adjusting for income changes
5. Not reviewing monthly

A budget is not set once.

It's reviewed monthly.

## Budgeting Tools

You can use:

- A notebook

- A spreadsheet
- Budgeting apps
- Bank tracking tools

The best system is the one you actually use.

Simplicity beats complexity.

## The 24-Hour Rule

For non-essential purchases over a set amount (for example $100):

Wait 24 hours.

Impulse fades.
Regret lasts.

This rule alone can save thousands per year.

## Budgeting and Confidence

When you know:

- Your income

- Your expenses
- Your savings rate
- Your goals

You stop feeling anxious about money.

Clarity reduces stress.

Control builds confidence.

Confidence changes decisions.

## Reflection Questions

1. Do I know my exact monthly net income?
2. What percentage of my income goes to savings?
3. Where do I overspend most often?
4. What expense could I reduce immediately?
5. If I earned 10% more, what would I do differently?

## Chapter Takeaway

Budgeting is not about restriction.

It's about direction.

When you budget:

- You reduce stress.
- You avoid debt.
- You build savings.
- You create options.

A boss doesn't guess.

A boss plans.

And when you control your money, you control your future.

CHAPTER 4

# BANKING 101

— Where Your Money Should Live

# Chapter 4: Banking 101 — Where Your Money Should Live

Making money is important.

Budgeting money is powerful.

But where you keep your money matters more than most people realize.

Not all accounts are equal.
Not all banks are equal.
And not all money should sit in the same place.

Your banking setup should work for you — not against you.

## The Purpose of a Bank

At its core, a bank does three things:

1. **Stores your money safely**
2. **Processes payments**
3. **Pays (or charges) interest**

But smart adults use banks strategically.

You don't just "have a bank account."

You build a system.

## Checking vs. Savings: Know the Difference

Many young adults mix everything together in one account.

That creates confusion and overspending.

### Checking Account

This is your transaction hub.

Use it for:

- Paying bills
- Debit card purchases
- Direct deposit
- ATM withdrawals

Checking accounts usually:

- Earn little or no interest
- Have easier access to funds
- May have monthly fees

Think of checking as your spending account.

**Savings Account**

This is for money you do not plan to spend regularly.

Use it for:

- Emergency fund
- Short-term savings
- Planned purchases

Savings accounts:

- Earn interest
- Limit monthly withdrawals (depending on bank policy)

- Help separate spending from saving

If your savings is in your checking account, it is not protected from you.

## High-Yield Savings Accounts (HYSA)

Traditional savings accounts often pay very little interest.

A High-Yield Savings Account (HYSA) pays significantly more.

Example:

If you save $5,000:

- Traditional savings may earn very little.
- HYSA earns more over time.

It won't make you rich.
But it helps your money grow while it sits.

Smart money earns something — even while waiting.

# Online Banks vs. Traditional Banks

There are two main types of banks:

### Traditional (Brick-and-Mortar)

- Physical branches
- In-person customer service
- Often higher fees
- Lower savings interest rates

### Online Banks

- No physical branches
- Higher interest rates
- Fewer fees
- Fully digital experience

Online banks often pass savings (from not operating buildings) to customers through better interest rates.

The best choice depends on your comfort level.

But understand:
Convenience should not cost you growth.

## Avoiding Bank Fees

Banks make money from:

- Overdraft fees
- Monthly maintenance fees
- ATM fees
- Late payment penalties

To avoid fees:

- Keep a small buffer in checking
- Turn off overdraft protection (if needed)
- Use in-network ATMs
- Read account terms

One $35 overdraft fee might not seem big.

But repeated mistakes can cost hundreds per year.

## Direct Deposit: Set It and Forget It

Direct deposit sends your paycheck straight to your account.

This allows you to automate:

- Savings transfers
- Investment contributions
- Bill payments

Automation removes the temptation to spend before saving.

The more automatic your system is, the less willpower you need.

## The Three-Account Strategy

A simple but powerful setup:

1. **Checking Account** – For bills and spending

2. **Savings Account** – For emergencies

3. **Growth Account** – Investments or retirement

Each account has a job.

When accounts have purpose, money has direction.

## Emergency Fund Placement

Your emergency fund should:

- Be easily accessible

- Earn interest

- Not be invested in volatile assets

Do not put emergency money in stocks.

Emergencies don't wait for the market to recover.

A High-Yield Savings Account is often ideal.

## Joint Accounts vs. Individual Accounts

If you share finances (spouse or partner):

Options include:

- Separate accounts
- Joint account
- Hybrid model (joint for bills, separate for personal spending)

The key is clarity and communication.

Financial stress often comes from confusion — not income level.

## Mobile Banking & Financial Awareness

Modern banking apps allow you to:

- Track transactions instantly
- Freeze cards

- Transfer funds
- Monitor balances daily

Check your account at least weekly.

Awareness prevents surprises.

Surprises create stress.

## The Danger of Keeping All Your Money in One Place

If all your money is in one checking account:

- You overspend easily
- You don't see progress
- You blur the line between spending and saving

Separation creates discipline.

Discipline builds wealth.

## Interest: The Bank Is Always Earning

Here's something important:

If your money earns 0.01% interest in checking, but your credit card charges 18–25% interest…

The bank is winning.

Understanding interest — both earned and charged — changes behavior.

You want to:

- Earn interest on savings.
- Avoid paying high interest on debt.

## Reflection Questions

1. Do I know the interest rate on my savings account?
2. Have I paid any bank fees in the last 6 months?

3. Is my emergency fund separate from spending money?

4. Could I automate more of my financial system?

## Chapter Takeaway

Your bank should be a tool.

Not a trap.

Not a storage unit for careless spending.

Where your money lives determines how it grows.

When your accounts are structured properly:

- Spending becomes intentional.
- Saving becomes automatic.
- Growth becomes consistent.

Smart banking is quiet. But powerful.

CHAPTER 5

# EMERGENCY FUNDS & FINANCIAL STABILITY

# Chapter 5: Emergency Funds & Financial Stability

Emergencies are not a matter of *if*.

They are a matter of *when*.

Car repairs.
Medical bills.
Job loss.
Family emergencies.
Unexpected travel.
Home repairs.

Life does not schedule problems around your paycheck.

An emergency fund is not optional.

It is protection.

## What Is an Emergency Fund?

An emergency fund is money set aside specifically for unexpected expenses.

It is not:

- Vacation money
- Shopping money
- Holiday spending
- Investment capital

It is financial shock absorption.

Without it, emergencies become debt.

With it, emergencies become inconvenience.

## Why Most People Stay Stressed

Financial stress usually comes from three things:

1. No savings
2. High debt
3. Unstable income

Even people with decent income feel anxious when thcy know:

"If something happens, I'm not prepared."

An emergency fund reduces anxiety.

It gives you breathing room.

It gives you time.

And time creates better decisions.

## How Much Should You Save?

There are two phases of emergency savings.

### Phase 1: Starter Emergency Fund

Goal: $1,000 – $2,000

This covers:

- Minor car repairs
- Small medical expenses
- Short-term emergencies

This is your immediate safety net.

Build this first — even before heavy investing.

### Phase 2: Full Emergency Fund

Goal: 3–6 months of essential expenses

Calculate:

- Rent or mortgage
- Utilities
- Insurance
- Food
- Transportation
- Minimum debt payments

If your essential expenses are $2,500 per month:

3 months = $7,500
6 months = $15,000

This is not excessive.

It is stability.

## Why 3–6 Months?

Because job loss is unpredictable.

Because recovery takes time.

Because stress makes people desperate.

An emergency fund allows you to:

- Leave toxic work environments
- Avoid high-interest debt
- Avoid borrowing from family
- Avoid panic decisions

Financial stability creates emotional stability.

## Where Should You Keep It?

Your emergency fund should be:

- Separate from checking
- Easily accessible
- In a safe account (not invested in stocks)

A high-yield savings account is ideal.

Do not invest emergency funds in volatile assets.

The market does not care that you have a car repair tomorrow.

## What Counts as an Emergency?

Ask yourself:

Is this unexpected?
Is this necessary?
Is this urgent?

Examples of real emergencies:

- Medical expenses
- Job loss
- Essential home repairs
- Major car breakdown

Not emergencies:

- Concert tickets
- Flash sales
- Vacations

- Impulse purchases

Discipline protects the fund.

## How to Build It Faster

Many people say:

“I can’t save.”

The truth is often:

“I haven’t prioritized saving.”

Here are practical strategies:

### 1. Automate It

Set up automatic transfers weekly or biweekly.

Even $50 per paycheck adds up.

### 2. Use Windfalls Wisely

Tax refunds
Bonuses
Gifts
Side hustle income

Instead of spending it all, split it:

50% emergency fund
50% other goals

### 3. Cut One Expense Temporarily

Cancel one subscription.
Reduce eating out.
Pause unnecessary spending.

Short-term discipline builds long-term security.

### 4. Increase Income Temporarily

Pick up overtime.
Take on a short-term gig.
Sell unused items.

Sometimes the fastest way to build savings is not cutting — it's earning.

## The Confidence Factor

An emergency fund changes how you walk into rooms.

You negotiate differently.
You handle stress differently.
You take smarter risks.

When you know:
"I'm covered."

Your mindset shifts.

You are no longer operating from fear.

You are operating from strategy.

## The Hidden Benefit: Breaking the Debt Cycle

Without emergency savings:

Car repair → Credit card

Medical bill → Personal loan

Appliance breaks → Financing

Debt becomes normal.

With emergency savings:

Car repair → Paid

Medical bill → Covered

Appliance → Replaced

No interest.
No stress.
No cycle.

Savings break cycles.

## The Stability Formula

Income + Budget + Emergency Fund = Stability

Without savings, income alone is fragile.

With savings, even moderate income becomes powerful.

Financial stability is not about looking rich.

It's about being prepared.

## Reflection Questions

1. Do I currently have a starter emergency fund?

2. How many months of expenses could I survive today?

3. What expense category could I reduce to build this faster?

4. What would change in my life if I had 6 months saved?

## Chapter Takeaway

An emergency fund is not exciting.

It doesn't post well on social media.
It doesn't impress anyone.

But it protects everything.

Financial stability is quiet.
It's disciplined.
It's intentional.

And it's one of the strongest foundations you can build.

CHAPTER 6

# CREDIT

— The Adult Report Card

# Chapter 6: Credit — The Adult Report Card

In school, your grades followed you.

In adulthood, your credit follows you.

It determines:

- Whether you get approved
- What interest rate you pay
- How much you pay over time
- Sometimes even where you live or work

Credit is not about money you have.

It's about how you handle money you borrow.

Think of it as your financial reputation.

## What Is a Credit Score?

A credit score is a three-digit number that represents how risky you are to lenders.

Most scores range from **300 to 850**.

General breakdown:

- 300–579: Poor
- 580–669: Fair
- 670–739: Good
- 740–799: Very Good
- 800–850: Excellent

The higher the score, the lower the risk you appear to lenders.

Lower risk = lower interest rates.

Lower interest rates = thousands saved.

## Why Credit Matters More Than You Think

Your credit can affect:

- Car loan approvals
- Mortgage rates
- Apartment applications

- Insurance premiums
- Credit card approvals
- Utility deposits

Two people can buy the same car.

One pays $450/month.
The other pays $650/month.

The difference?
Credit.

Over time, bad credit becomes expensive.

## How Credit Scores Are Calculated

Your score is based on five main factors:

### 1. Payment History (35%)

Do you pay on time?

One missed payment can drop your score significantly.

Consistency builds trust.

### 2. Credit Utilization (30%)

How much of your available credit are you using?

Example:
Credit limit: $1,000
Balance: $800

That's 80% utilization — too high.

Experts recommend staying below 30%.

Lower is better.

### 3. Length of Credit History (15%)

How long have your accounts been open?

Older accounts help your score.

Closing your oldest credit card can sometimes hurt you.

### 4. Credit Mix (10%)

Do you have different types of credit?

- Credit cards
- Auto loans

- Student loans
- Mortgages

A healthy mix shows responsibility.

### 5. New Credit Inquiries (10%)

Applying for too many accounts in a short period lowers your score temporarily.

Each application triggers a “hard inquiry.”

Too many = red flag.

## Credit Cards: Tool or Trap?

Credit cards are not evil.

But they are powerful.

Used properly, they:

- Build credit
- Offer fraud protection
- Provide rewards

- Help establish history

Used poorly, they:

- Accumulate high interest (18–25%+)
- Lead to debt cycles
- Lower your score

The rule:

If you can't pay it off monthly,
don't swipe it.

## Interest: The Silent Wealth Killer

Example:

You carry a $3,000 balance at 22% interest.
You only make minimum payments.

You could pay thousands in interest alone.

Interest works two ways:

- Against you in debt
- For you in investing

Your goal:
Avoid high-interest debt.
Earn interest, don't pay it.

## How to Build Credit the Right Way

If you're starting from scratch:

### 1. Get a Secured Credit Card

You deposit money (example: $300).
That becomes your limit.

Use lightly.
Pay in full monthly.

### 2. Become an Authorized User

A trusted family member adds you to their card.

Their positive history may help your score.

### 3. Keep Utilization Low

Even if your limit is $1,000,
don't carry more than $300.

Lower balances show control.

### 4. Pay On Time — Every Time

Set up automatic payments.

Late payments stay on your report for years.

Consistency is everything.

## Common Credit Mistakes

- Maxing out cards
- Ignoring statements
- Missing payments by a few days
- Closing old accounts too soon
- Applying for multiple cards quickly
- Co-signing without understanding risk

Co-signing means:
If they don't pay,
you pay.

Your score suffers too.

## Bad Credit Is Not Permanent

If you've made mistakes:

- Pay all bills on time moving forward
- Lower balances
- Avoid new debt
- Dispute errors on your report

Credit can be rebuilt.

It takes time.
But time passes anyway.

## The Long-Term Impact

Let's compare two people:

Person A:
Credit score 750
Auto loan rate: 5%

Person B:
Credit score 600
Auto loan rate: 15%

On a $25,000 car,
Person B could pay thousands more in interest.

Credit is expensive when neglected.

But powerful when managed.

## Credit and Discipline

Credit rewards consistency.

It doesn’t care about:

- Your intentions
- Your excuses
- Your stress

It responds to behavior.

Responsible behavior builds access.

Access builds opportunity.

## Reflection Questions

1. Do I know my current credit score?

2. Have I missed any payments in the last year?
3. What is my current credit utilization percentage?
4. Do I use credit strategically or emotionally?

## Chapter Takeaway

Credit is your adult report card.

It tells lenders one thing:

Can you be trusted?

High income without discipline leads to bad credit.

Moderate income with discipline builds strong credit.

And strong credit lowers the cost of your life.

Handle it wisely.

CHAPTER 7

# DEBT

— When It Helps and When It Hurts

# Chapter 7: Debt — When It Helps and When It Hurts

Debt is not the enemy.

Uncontrolled debt is.

Most young adults are told one of two extreme messages:

- "All debt is bad."
- "Debt is normal — everyone has it."

The truth is more strategic.

Debt is a tool.

And like any tool, it can build something — or destroy something.

## What Is Debt?

Debt is borrowed money that must be repaid — usually with interest.

When you borrow:
You are using tomorrow's money today.

The question is:

Is tomorrow stronger because of it?
Or weaker?

## Good Debt vs. Bad Debt

The difference is not emotional.

It's mathematical.

### Good Debt

Good debt has the potential to increase your income or net worth over time.

Examples:

- Education that increases earning potential
- A mortgage on a property that builds equity
- Business loans that create revenue

Good debt should:

- Have reasonable interest
- Create long-term value
- Be manageable within your income

Good debt builds assets.

### Bad Debt

Bad debt loses value or does not generate income.

Examples:

- High-interest credit cards
- Expensive car loans you can't afford
- Financing consumer goods
- Buy-now-pay-later purchases

Bad debt:

- Carries high interest
- Depreciates quickly

- Creates stress
- Limits flexibility

Bad debt finances lifestyle.
Good debt finances growth.

## The Interest Trap

Interest is the price of borrowing.

If you borrow $5,000 at 20% interest,
you are not paying back $5,000.

You are paying back much more.

The higher the interest rate:
The more expensive your life becomes.

High-interest debt steals from your future.

## Student Loans: Investment or Burden?

Education can increase earning potential.

But student loans must be strategic.

Before borrowing, ask:

- What is the expected starting salary?
- What is the total loan amount?
- What will monthly payments be?
- Can I realistically afford this?

A $30,000 loan for a career earning $70,000? Possibly strategic.

A $120,000 loan for a career earning $40,000? Risky.

Education should increase opportunity — not create lifelong strain.

## Car Loans: The Silent Budget Killer

Cars depreciate quickly.

That means they lose value over time.

If you finance a $35,000 vehicle with high interest, you may end up paying $45,000+ for something worth much less later.

Transportation is necessary.

Luxury transportation is optional.

Drive what supports your goals — not your ego.

## The Debt-to-Income Ratio (DTI)

Your DTI measures how much of your income goes toward debt payments.

Formula:

Monthly debt payments ÷ Monthly gross income = DTI

Example:

$1,000 debt payments
$4,000 income

DTI = 25%

Lenders prefer lower DTI ratios.

Lower debt = higher flexibility.

## How Debt Affects Your Freedom

Debt reduces options.

High payments mean:

- You can't take career risks.
- You can't move easily.
- You can't invest aggressively.
- You feel pressure constantly.

Financial freedom is not about income alone.

It's about low obligations.

## Debt Payoff Strategies

If you have debt, you need a strategy.

### 1. Debt Snowball Method

Pay smallest balance first.
Gain momentum.
Roll payments into next debt.

Psychological wins build motivation.

### 2. Debt Avalanche Method

Pay highest interest rate first.
Saves more money long-term.

Mathematical advantage.

Both work.

The best method is the one you will consistently follow.

## Avoiding Future Debt

Before taking on new debt, ask:

1. Is this increasing my income?
2. Is this building an asset?
3. Can I pay it off quickly?
4. Would I still do this if no one could see it?

Many debt decisions are emotional.

Discipline creates distance between emotion and action.

## The Debt-Free Advantage

Imagine:

No credit card payments.
No car note.
Minimal obligations.

Your income becomes powerful.

You can:

- Invest more
- Save more
- Take career risks
- Build businesses
- Travel without stress

Debt-free living is quiet wealth.

## When Debt Helps

Debt can help when:

- You are investing in income-producing assets.

- You are purchasing appreciating assets.
- You have a stable repayment plan.
- The interest rate is reasonable.

Used wisely, debt can accelerate growth.

Used recklessly, it delays it.

## Reflection Questions

1. What debts do I currently have?
2. What is the interest rate on each?
3. Which debts are helping me grow?
4. Which debts are holding me back?
5. What is my payoff plan?

## Chapter Takeaway

Debt is not evil.

But it demands respect.

Borrowing should be strategic — not emotional.

Before signing anything, ask:

Will this decision make my future stronger?

Because every dollar borrowed today
either builds your future —

or limits it.

CHAPTER 8

# INVESTING

— Make Your Money Work

# Chapter 8: Investing — Make Your Money Work

Most people trade time for money.

Investors make money work for time.

If you only earn and save, you grow slowly.

If you earn, save, **and invest**, you build wealth.

Investing is not gambling.
It is ownership.

When you invest, you buy pieces of businesses, assets, or systems that generate returns.

The earlier you start, the more powerful it becomes.

## Why Saving Alone Isn't Enough

Saving protects money.

Investing grows money.

If you keep $10,000 in a regular savings account earning very little,

it barely grows.

But if that same $10,000 is invested over time, it can grow significantly through compounding.

Inflation reduces purchasing power.

Investing helps you outpace inflation.

## The Power of Compound Interest

Compound interest means you earn returns on:

- Your original money
- The returns that money already made

It's growth on top of growth.

Example:

If you invest $200 per month starting at age 22,
and earn an average return over time,
you could build substantial wealth by retirement.

If you wait until 32 to start,
you must invest much more to catch up.

Time matters more than amount.

Start early.
Stay consistent.

## What Can You Invest In?

There are many investment options.

The key is understanding what you own.

### 1. Stocks

When you buy a stock, you own a small piece of a company.

If the company grows and becomes more valuable,
your shares increase in value.

Stocks can rise and fall in the short term,
but historically grow over long periods.

### 2. Index Funds & ETFs

An index fund or ETF (Exchange-Traded Fund) holds many companies inside one investment.

Instead of picking one company,
you buy a basket.

This spreads risk.

For beginners, index funds are often a simple and effective strategy.

### 3. Retirement Accounts

Two common types:

**401(k)**

- Offered through employers
- May include employer match (free money)
- Contributions reduce taxable income

If your employer offers a match, contribute enough to get it.
Not doing so leaves money on the table.

**Roth IRA**

- Funded with after-tax money
- Growth and withdrawals in retirement can be tax-free (if rules are followed)
- Flexible for young investors

Many young adults benefit from starting a Roth IRA early.

### 4. Real Estate

Real estate can generate:

- Rental income
- Appreciation
- Tax advantages

It requires more capital and responsibility, but can build long-term wealth.

## Risk and Return

All investing involves risk.

Higher potential returns usually mean higher risk.

But risk decreases with:

- Diversification
- Long-term thinking
- Consistency

- Education

Short-term investing is speculation.

Long-term investing is strategy.

## The Biggest Investing Mistakes

1. Waiting too long to start
2. Trying to "time the market"
3. Investing emotionally
4. Following hype without research
5. Selling during market drops

Markets rise and fall.

Long-term investors focus on decades, not days.

## Starting with Small Amounts

You do not need thousands to begin.

You can start with:

- $25
- $50
- $100 per month

Consistency matters more than size.

Small investments compound into large results over time.

## The Ownership Mindset

Spenders buy products.

Investors buy ownership.

Instead of only buying from companies,
consider owning pieces of them.

When companies grow,
owners benefit.

That shift in thinking changes everything.

## Automate Investing

Just like savings,
investing should be automated.

Set up:

- Automatic retirement contributions
- Automatic Roth IRA deposits
- Automatic investment transfers

Automation removes emotion.

Emotion causes panic.

## Market Drops: What to Do

When markets fall:

- Do not panic.
- Do not sell impulsively.
- Continue investing if possible.

Market drops often create opportunity.

Long-term wealth is built through patience.

## The Wealth Gap Is Often an Investing Gap

Two people earn the same salary.

One spends and saves only.

One spends, saves, and invests.

Over 20–30 years, the difference can be dramatic.

Income creates opportunity.

Investing multiplies it.

## Reflection Questions

1. Do I currently invest?

2. Am I taking advantage of employer retirement benefits?

3. What percentage of my income goes toward investing?

4. If I start investing today, what will my future self thank me for?

## Chapter Takeaway

Investing is not reserved for the wealthy.

It is how people become wealthy.

You do not need to be an expert.

You need to be consistent.

Make your money work.

Let time do its job.

And remember:

The earlier you start,
the less you have to stress later.

CHAPTER 9

# ENTREPRENEURSHIP & SIDE HUSTLES

— Entrepreneurship & Side Hustles

# Chapter 9: Entrepreneurship & Side Hustles

A job can pay your bills.

A career can grow your income.

Entrepreneurship can change your ceiling.

You don't need to quit your job tomorrow.
You don't need a viral idea.
You don't need investors.

You need value.

Entrepreneurship is simply solving problems for profit.

Side hustles are the training ground.

## Why Side Hustles Matter

Most people rely on one income stream.

That is risky.

If that one stream stops, everything stops.

Multiple income streams provide:

- Security
- Flexibility
- Faster debt payoff
- Faster investing
- More confidence

One income maintains life.
Multiple incomes build wealth.

## What Is a Side Hustle?

A side hustle is income earned outside your primary job.

It can be:

- Skill-based
- Product-based
- Service-based
- Digital

- Physical
- Creative

The key difference between a hobby and a side hustle?

A hobby costs you.
A side hustle pays you.

## Turning Skills into Income

You already have something valuable.

Ask yourself:

- What do people compliment me on?
- What do people ask me for help with?
- What do I do naturally that others struggle with?

Examples:

Good at design? → Graphic services

Good with numbers? → Bookkeeping or tutoring

Good with tools? → Handyman services

Good at organizing? → Consulting or coaching

Skills are assets.

Monetize them.

## Digital Opportunities

Technology has lowered the barrier to entry.

You can earn through:

- Freelance platforms
- Selling digital products
- E-commerce
- Content creation
- Online tutoring
- Consulting

Digital businesses often require low startup costs.

Time and consistency matter more than money upfront.

## The Power of Branding

People don't just buy products.

They buy trust.

Branding includes:

- Clear identity
- Professional presentation
- Consistent messaging
- Reliability

Even a small side hustle should look serious.

Presentation increases perceived value.

And perceived value increases price.

## Start Small, Scale Smart

Many people fail because they try to scale before proving demand.

Start by:

1. Testing your idea
2. Serving a small group
3. Collecting feedback
4. Refining your process
5. Raising prices strategically

Growth should follow proof. Not excitement.

## Pricing: Respect Your Value

Underpricing is common.

People charge too little because they fear rejection.

But pricing should reflect:

- Skill level
- Time invested

- Market demand
- Value delivered

Low prices attract price-sensitive customers.

Fair prices attract serious clients.

## The Time Management Reality

Side hustles require discipline.

You must:

- Manage your time wisely
- Protect your energy
- Stay consistent
- Avoid burnout

Schedule your hustle like an appointment.

Consistency builds momentum.

## When a Side Hustle Becomes a Business

A side hustle becomes a business when:

- It generates consistent income
- It operates beyond your direct hours
- It has systems
- It can scale

At that point, you shift from:

"I make extra money."

To:

"I own an asset."

Ownership builds wealth.

## The Risk Factor

Entrepreneurship involves risk.

Income may fluctuate.
Clients may leave.
Demand may change.

But risk decreases with:

- Emergency savings
- Budget discipline
- Skill development
- Diversified income streams

Never quit stability without preparation.

Smart risk is calculated.

## Reinvesting Profits

When you earn from a side hustle:

Avoid immediately upgrading your lifestyle.

Instead:

- Reinvest into the business
- Pay down debt
- Increase investments
- Build savings

Profit should build leverage.

Not just purchases.

## The Long-Term Vision

Entrepreneurship is not about quick money.

It is about:

- Ownership
- Scalability
- Impact
- Legacy

Even if your side hustle never replaces your job, it can:

- Fund investments
- Accelerate debt payoff
- Build confidence
- Create opportunities

And sometimes,
it becomes something bigger than you imagined.

## Reflection Questions

1. What skill do I have that could generate income?

2. What problem can I solve?

3. How many income streams do I currently have?

4. What would an extra $500 per month change in my life?

5. What is stopping me from starting?

## Chapter Takeaway

Entrepreneurship is leverage.

Side hustles are an opportunity.

You don't have to choose between employment and ownership.

You can build both.

Income covers expenses.

Investing builds wealth.

Entrepreneurship expands possibilities.

And when you combine all three —

you stop thinking about survival
and start thinking about freedom.

CHAPTER 10

# INSURANCE & PROTECTION

— Insurance & Protection

# Chapter 10: Insurance & Protection

Most people don't think about insurance until something goes wrong.

An accident.
An illness.
A lawsuit.
A disaster.

Insurance feels unnecessary — until it becomes urgent.

The purpose of insurance is simple:

Protect what you've built.

You work hard to earn.
You budget carefully.
You save intentionally.
You invest strategically.

Insurance protects all of it.

## What Is Insurance?

Insurance is a financial agreement.

You pay a small, predictable amount (a premium) to avoid a large, unpredictable loss.

It transfers risk from you to an insurance company.

Without insurance:
One major event can wipe out years of progress.

With insurance:
You limit damage.

## Health Insurance

Medical costs can be overwhelming.

Even a short hospital visit can cost thousands.

Health insurance helps cover:

- Doctor visits
- Prescriptions
- Emergency care
- Surgeries
- Preventive services

Without it, a medical emergency can turn into long-term debt.

Even if you're young and healthy, protection matters.

Health issues don't check your age first.

## Auto Insurance

If you drive, you need auto insurance.

Most states require at least liability coverage.

Auto insurance can cover:

- Damage to your vehicle
- Damage to other vehicles
- Medical expenses
- Legal costs

Driving without insurance is risky — financially and legally.

A single accident without coverage can create long-term financial strain.

## Renters Insurance

Many renters skip this.

That's a mistake.

If there's a fire, theft, or water damage,
your landlord's insurance does not cover your belongings.

Renters insurance is often inexpensive and protects:

- Furniture
- Electronics
- Clothing
- Personal property

Small cost.
Big protection.

## Homeowners Insurance

If you own a home, this is essential.

It protects:

- The structure
- Personal belongings
- Liability
- Natural disasters (depending on policy)

Your home is likely one of your largest assets.

Protect it properly.

## Life Insurance

Life insurance protects people who depend on your income.

If someone relies on you financially — spouse, child, parent —
life insurance ensures they are supported if something happens to you.

Two main types:

### Term Life Insurance

- Covers a specific time period
- Lower cost
- Simple protection

### Whole Life Insurance

- Permanent coverage
- More expensive
- Includes investment components

For most young adults with families, term insurance is often practical and affordable.

Insurance is not for you.

It's for the people you leave behind.

## Disability Insurance

Your ability to earn income is your greatest asset.

If you cannot work due to injury or illness, disability insurance replaces a portion of your income.

Many employers offer some coverage, but it may not be enough.

Protecting your income is just as important as protecting property.

## Deductibles and Premiums

Two important terms:

**Premium**

The monthly or yearly amount you pay for coverage.

**Deductible**

The amount you pay out of pocket before insurance begins covering costs.

Lower premium = usually higher deductible.
Higher premium = usually lower deductible.

Choose based on your savings and risk tolerance.

## The Danger of Being Underinsured

Some people choose the cheapest coverage without understanding limits.

Low coverage can leave you exposed.

For example:
If your policy covers $25,000 in liability,
but you cause $75,000 in damages,
you may owe the difference.

Understand what your policy covers.

Cheap coverage isn't always smart coverage.

## Insurance and Wealth Protection

Think of insurance as defense.

Budgeting and investing are offense.

You need both.

Wealth isn't just about growth.

It's about protection.

## When to Review Coverage

Life changes mean insurance needs change.

Review your coverage when:

- You get married
- You have children
- You buy a home

- Your income increases
- You start a business

As your life grows, your protection should grow too.

## The Mindset Shift

Some people say:

“I don’t want to pay for something I may never use.”

But that’s the point.

Insurance is successful when you don’t need it.

It exists for worst-case scenarios.

It protects your long-term plan from short-term disasters.

## Reflection Questions

1. Do I currently have health insurance?
2. Is my vehicle properly insured?
3. If something happened to me tomorrow, would my family be financially secure?
4. Do I understand my deductibles and coverage limits?

## Chapter Takeaway

Insurance is not exciting.

It doesn't create wealth directly.

But it protects everything you are building.

Wealth without protection is fragile.

Protection turns effort into stability.

Stability turns income into freedom.

And freedom allows you to build confidently.

CHAPTER 11

# ADULT MILESTONES

## — Cars, Apartments & First Homes

# Chapter 11: Adult Milestones — Cars, Apartments & First Homes

Adulthood isn't announced.

It shows up in contracts.

A car loan.
An apartment lease.
A mortgage application.

These are milestone moments — and expensive ones.

The decisions you make here can either:

Build your financial future
or
Delay it.

This chapter is about moving wisely.

# Milestone #1: Buying a Car

For many young adults, a car is the first major financial commitment.

Transportation is necessary.

But the *type* of transportation is a choice.

## New vs. Used

New cars:

- Higher price
- Rapid depreciation
- Higher insurance
- Warranty protection

Used cars:

- Lower cost
- Slower depreciation

- Often more affordable insurance

Cars lose value quickly.

That means financing a brand-new car with a long loan term can be financially heavy.

Drive what supports your goals — not your image.

### The Monthly Payment Trap

Many buyers focus only on the monthly payment.

Instead, ask:

- What is the total price?
- What is the interest rate?
- What is the total paid over the life of the loan?

A lower monthly payment over a longer term often means more interest paid.

The goal:
Affordable payment.
Reasonable interest.
Shorter loan term if possible.

### Insurance and Maintenance

Before buying a car, calculate:

- Insurance cost
- Gas
- Maintenance
- Registration
- Repairs

The purchase price is only the beginning.

## Milestone #2: Renting Your First Apartment

Renting is often the first taste of independence.

But leases are legal contracts.

Read before signing.

## Understanding the Lease

A lease includes:

- Monthly rent
- Lease length
- Security deposit
- Late fees
- Maintenance responsibilities
- Penalties for breaking the lease

Once signed, you are legally responsible.

Make sure the payment fits comfortably in your budget.

## The 30% Rule

A common guideline:

Housing should not exceed 30% of your gross income.

Example:

If you earn $4,000 per month (gross),
aim for rent around $1,200 or less.

Higher housing costs reduce flexibility.

Lower housing costs increase opportunity.

**Hidden Costs of Renting**

Beyond rent, consider:

- Utilities
- Internet
- Parking fees
- Renter's insurance
- Furnishing costs

Independence costs more than just rent.

Plan accordingly.

## Milestone #3: Buying Your First Home

Homeownership is often seen as a symbol of success.

But it is both a financial and lifestyle decision.

### Renting vs. Buying

Renting:

- Flexibility
- Lower upfront costs
- Less maintenance responsibility

Buying:

- Builds equity

- Potential appreciation
- Stability
- Responsibility for repairs

Neither is automatically better.

The right decision depends on:

- Income stability
- Savings
- Location
- Long-term plans

## Down Payment & Closing Costs

Buying a home requires:

- Down payment (often 3–20%)
- Closing costs
- Inspection fees

- Appraisal fees

Owning also includes:

- Property taxes
- Homeowners insurance
- Maintenance

Homeownership is not just a mortgage payment.

It's full responsibility.

## Equity: Why It Matters

When you make mortgage payments, part of it builds equity.

Equity = ownership stake in your property.

Over time, equity can:

- Increase net worth
- Provide borrowing power
- Create financial leverage

But only if purchased wisely.

## Avoiding Financial Regret

Before any major milestone purchase, ask:

1. Does this fit within my budget comfortably?
2. Will this decision reduce my ability to save or invest?
3. Am I buying for stability or appearance?
4. Could I wait and strengthen my position?

Patience often leads to better deals.

Impulse often leads to regret.

## Lifestyle Inflation and Milestones

As income increases, many people upgrade everything at once:

- New apartment
- New car
- New furniture
- Higher expenses

Upgrading too quickly can eliminate the benefits of income growth.

Grow your lifestyle slowly.
Grow your assets consistently.

## The Long-Term View

A car is transportation.

An apartment is shelter.

A home can be an asset.

But none of them define you.

Financial maturity is not about having the biggest house or newest car.

It's about:

Affordability
Flexibility
Peace of mind

## Reflection Questions

1. If I lost my income tomorrow, could I maintain my current housing?

2. Am I prioritizing appearance over affordability?

3. What milestone am I financially preparing for next?

4. How can I strengthen my financial position before signing a major contract?

## Chapter Takeaway

Adult milestones come with responsibility.

Cars, apartments, and homes are not just purchases.

They are commitments.

When approached wisely, they build stability.

When rushed, they create pressure.

Your goal is not just to move forward.

It is to move forward strategically.

Because financial freedom is not about how fast you upgrade.

It's about how wisely you build.

CHAPTER 12

# WEALTH, OWNERSHIP & GENERATIONAL IMPACT

— Wealth, Ownership & Generational Impact

# Chapter 12: Wealth, Ownership & Generational Impact

Money is not the goal.

Freedom is.

Security is.

Opportunity is.

Impact is.

Throughout this book, you've learned how to:

- Earn income
- Budget intentionally
- Protect yourself
- Use credit wisely
- Eliminate harmful debt
- Invest strategically
- Build additional income

Now we step into something bigger.

Wealth.

## What Wealth Really Is

Wealth is not income.

Wealth is not flashy purchases.

Wealth is ownership.

Wealth is assets that produce income without constant labor.

Examples of wealth:

- Investments that grow
- Rental properties that produce cash flow
- Businesses that generate revenue
- Retirement accounts compounding over time
- Intellectual property that earns royalties

Income pays bills.

Ownership builds freedom.

## Assets vs. Liabilities

Understanding this difference changes everything.

### Assets

Put money in your pocket.

Examples:

- Stocks
- Index funds
- Rental property
- Businesses
- Cash-flowing investments

### Liabilities

Take money out of your pocket.

Examples:

- Car loans

- Credit card debt
- Consumer purchases
- Expensive obligations

The wealthy focus on acquiring assets.

The average consumer focuses on upgrading liabilities.

Your net worth grows when assets grow.

## The Ownership Mindset

Consumers ask:
"What can I buy?"

Owners ask:
"What can I build?"

Consumers spend bonuses.

Owners invest bonuses.

Consumers finance lifestyle.

Owners finance opportunity.

Ownership requires patience.

But it creates leverage.

## The 10-Year Vision

Instead of asking:

“What do I want this year?”

Ask:

“Where do I want to be in 10 years?”

Consider:

- What assets will I own?
- How many income streams will I have?
- How much invested capital will I control?
- Will I still be trading only time for money?

Wealth is built in decades — not months.

Time rewards discipline.

## Breaking the Cycle

Many families pass down:

- Hard work
- Resilience
- Determination

But sometimes also:

- Financial stress
- Debt cycles
- Lack of investing knowledge
- Fear of ownership

You can be the turning point.

Building wealth is not just about you.

It changes:

- Your children's opportunities
- Your family's stability
- Your future options

Generational impact begins with one disciplined decision at a time.

## Teaching the Next Generation

Wealth that isn't understood is often lost.

True generational wealth includes:

- Financial education
- Strong habits
- Ownership principles
- Investment knowledge
- Responsibility

Teach:

- Budgeting early
- Saving consistently
- Investing patiently
- Avoiding unnecessary debt

Money without wisdom disappears.

Wisdom sustains wealth.

## Giving and Impact

Wealth is not only about accumulation.

It's about contribution.

When you are financially stable, you can:

- Support family members
- Invest in community
- Fund opportunities for others
- Give without harming your own stability

Generosity is strongest when it is structured.

Give from overflow — not from pressure.

## Financial Independence

Financial independence does not mean you never work.

It means you don't have to.

It means your assets generate enough to support your lifestyle.

That level of freedom:

- Reduces stress
- Increases options
- Expands opportunity

It may take time.

But every investment, every disciplined choice, moves you closer.

## Your Financial Blueprint

At this point, your blueprint should include:

1. Multiple income streams
2. A clear budget
3. Emergency savings

4. Strong credit
5. Controlled debt
6. Consistent investing
7. Protection through insurance
8. Intentional asset building

This is not complicated.

It is consistent.

## The Long Game

The world encourages:

Fast money.
Fast upgrades.
Fast results.

Wealth rewards:

Patience.
Discipline.
Ownership.
Long-term thinking.

Quiet builders often win.

Not because they are lucky.

But because they are consistent.

## Reflection Questions

1. What assets do I currently own?
2. What is my 10-year wealth vision?
3. What habits must I improve to reach that vision?
4. What financial lesson do I want to pass down?
5. Am I building something that will outlive me?

## Final Takeaway

Wealth is not accidental.

It is intentional.

It is built slowly.
Protected carefully.
Grown consistently.
Passed down wisely.

You don't need to start perfect.

You need to start aware.

The decisions you make today determine:

Not just your lifestyle —

But your legacy.

And legacy begins the moment you choose ownership over impulse,
discipline over pressure, and long-term freedom over short-term image.

Made in the USA
Monee, IL
19 April 2026

48591224R00100